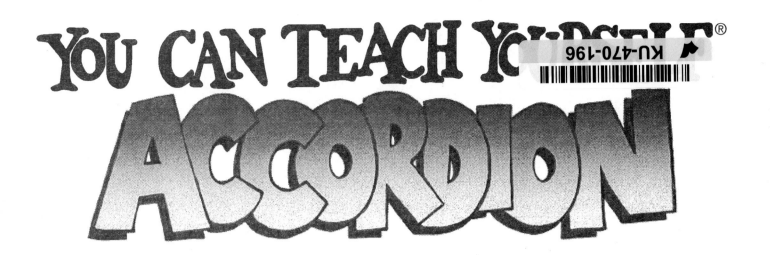

YOU CAN TEACH YOURSELF® ACCORDION

KU-470-196

by Neil Griffin

Photos courtesy of Hohner and Castiglione

CD Contents

1. Learning the C's (:19)
2. Putting the C's Together (:54)
3. Adding the G's (:16)
4. Mixing the C's and G's (:48)
5. Adding D, E, and F (:20)
6. Put it All Together (:48)
7. Bass and Chord Rhythm Drill (1:07)
8. *Oom-Pah-Pah Waltz* (:37)
9. *Everybody Has Their Ups and Downs* (:35)
10. New G Hand Position (:27)
11. *Déja Vu in G* (:34)
12. *Children's Song* (:44)
13. Learning Eighth Notes (:32)
14. *Minuet* (1:06)
15. *Ode to Joy* (:55)
16. *Air* (:39)
17. *Gavotte* (1:38)
18. *The British Grenadiers* (:36)
19. Alternating the Bass Notes (:31)
20. *Amazing Grace* (:39)
21. Key Signatures (1:03)
22. *Lullaby* (:32)
23. Introducing the Minor Chords (:30)
24. *Hungarian Dance #4* (:46)
25. Introducing the 7th Chords (:31)
26. *The God of Abraham Praise* (:49)
27. *Skaters Waltz* (:31)
28. *French Song* (:52)
29. *Sur le Pont d'Avignon* (:51)
30. *Wandering* (:30)
31. *The Bells of St. Marys* (:52)
32. *Polka, Polka* (1:02)
33. *Are You from Dixie* (:57)
34. *Lake Charles Waltz* (1:03)
35. *6/8 Time* (:26)
36. *When Johnny Comes Marching Home* (:39)
37. *Come Back to Sorrento* (1:31)
38. *Two Steppin' 'Cross Texas* (1:05)
39. *Julida Polka* (:31)
40. *Andante* (1:06)
41. *Jambalaya* (1:07)
42. *Pretty Fair Maid Jig* (1:33)
43. *Peg o' My Heart* (:44)
44. *Rattle the Bottles Reel* (:48)
45. *Rick's Reel* (:49)
46. Introducing the Counter-Bass Notes (:17)
47. Counter-Bass Notes-2 (:14)
48. Counter-Bass Notes-3 (:55)
49. *March* (1:30)
50. Introducing the Diminished Chords (:26)
51. *Ja-da* (:40)
52. *Chinatown* (1:02)
53. *I Want a Girl, Just Like the Girl* (1:08)
54. *I Love You Truly* (:59)
55. *Smiles* (1:06)
56. *For Me and My Gal* (1:05)
57. *Washington and Lee Swing* (1:01)
58. *Fascination* (1:10)
59. *El Capitan March* (1:15)
60. *Sweetheart of Sigma Chi* (1:11)
61. *Melancholy Baby* (1:20)
62. *El Caballo Bayo* (1:50)
63. *Mexican Siesta* (1:16)

---

2 3 4 5 6 7 8 9 0

MEL BAY®

Visit us on the Web at http://www.melbay.com — E-mail us at email@melbay.com

CONTENTS

Parts of the Accordion 3
About the Accordion 3
Holding the Accordion 4
Reference Section 5
The Left Hand 9
The Right Hand 11
Learning the C's 13
Adding the G's 15
Proper Use of the Bellows 16
The Tie 18
Bass and Chord Rhythm Drill 19
Oom-Pah-Pah Waltz 20
Everybody Has Their Ups and Down 21
New G Hand Position 22
Déja Vu in G 23
Repeat Sign 24
D.C. al Fine 24
Children's Song 24
Notes and Rests 25
Learning Eighth Notes 25
Minuet 26
Dotted Quarter Note 27
Ode to Joy 27
The Slur 28
Air 28
New C Hand Position 29
Gavotte 29
The British Grenadiers 30
Alternating the Bass Notes 31
The Triplet 32
Amazing Grace 32
Chromatics 33
Flats 34
Naturals 34
Key Signatures 35
Sustained Bass Notes 36
Lullaby 36
Introducing the Minor Chords 37
Relative Minor Keys 38
Hungarian Dance #4 39
Introducing the 7th Chords 40
The God of Abraham Praise 41
Skaters Waltz 42

French Song 43
Sur le Pont d'Avignon 44
Wandering 45
The Bells of St. Marys 46
Sixteenth Notes 47
Eighth Rest 47
Polka, Polka 47
Are You from Dixie 48
Grace Notes 50
Lake Charles Waltz 50
6/8 Time 52
When Johnny Comes Marching Home 53
Come Back to Sorrento 54
Dotted Eighths and Sixteenths 56
Two Steppin' 'Cross Texas 56
Julida Polka 58
Staccato 59
Legato 59
Andante 59
Jambalaya 60
Pretty Fair Maid Jig 62
Peg o' My Heart 63
Rattle the Bottles Reel 64
Rick's Reel 65
Introducing the Counter-Bass Notes 66
March 69
Introducing the Diminished Chords 70
Ja-da 71
Chinatown 72
I Want a Girl, Just Like the Girl 74
I Love You Truly 76
Smiles 78
For Me and My Gal 80
Washington and Lee Swing 82
Fascination 84
El Capitan March 86
Sweetheart of Sigma Chi 88
Melancholy Baby 90
Right-Hand Harmony 92
El Caballo Bayo 92
Mexican Siesta 94
Bass and Chord Button Review 96

PARTS OF THE ACCORDION

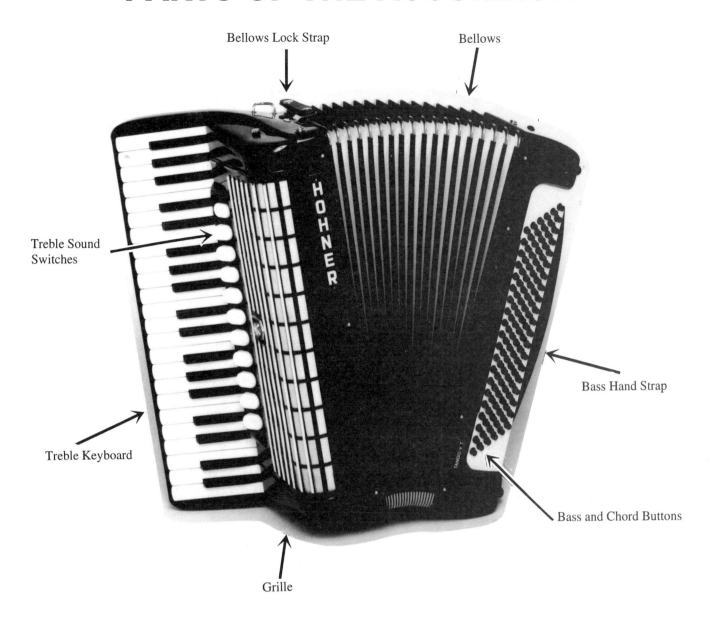

Bellows Lock Strap

Bellows

Treble Sound Switches

Treble Keyboard

Bass Hand Strap

Bass and Chord Buttons

Grille

ABOUT THE ACCORDION

The accordion is one of the world's most complete musical instruments. Why? Because it provides all the main ingredients — bass, harmony, and melody — all at the same time.

Although a little extra coordination is required, the accordion is probably one of the easiest musical instruments to learn to play. It is, of course, the predecessor of the chord organ and the electric keyboards that are so popular today.

The accordion is a "personal" type of instrument which continues to be enjoyed by thousands of people of widely varied ethnic origins. Think about it — French Canadian, Cajun, Tex-Mex, Irish, German, Italian, Spanish, Polish, etc., etc., etc.…

When the batteries run down or electricity is not readily available, or everyone begins to tire of all the synthetically produced music…

PICK UP YOUR ACCORDION AND "SMILE."

HOLDING THE ACCORDION

**HOLDING THE ACCORDION CORRECTLY – WHETHER STANDING
OR SITTING AFFECTS BOTH APPEARANCE AND PERFORMANCE.**

NOTICE THE FOLLOWING IMPORTANT POINTS
DEMONSTRATED IN THE ABOVE PHOTO.

THE KEYBOARD IS ONLY A FEW INCHES BELOW THE CHIN.

THE BLACK KEYS ARE DIRECTLY IN LINE UNDER THE CHIN
AND VERTICAL WITH THE CENTER LINE OF THE BODY.

THE BACK STRAPS ARE ADJUSTED TIGHTLY, PREVENTING THE ACCORDION FROM
MOVING SIDE TO SIDE WHEN THE BELLOWS ARE OPENED AND CLOSED.

REFERENCE SECTION

So that you will have a central place to refer to concerning musical information and specific explanations about mechanical as well as musical aspects of the accordion — several pages of illustrations and/or charts are included at this point.

Don't try to memorize all of this — just read through it and, as you proceed through this "Teach Yourself Method," it will be available to help you at any time.

Grey shaded boxes will appear throughout this book explaining and/or illustrating each new item as it is needed to play the next tune(s) correctly.

You are strongly advised to use this material in the order it is presented. Of course, a qualified teacher is helpful if available in your area.

HERE WE GO!

120-Bass Accordion

Notes

This is a note: ♪   A note has three parts. They are: the HEAD   ●

the STEM |

the FLAG   ♪

Notes may be placed in the staff,   above the staff,

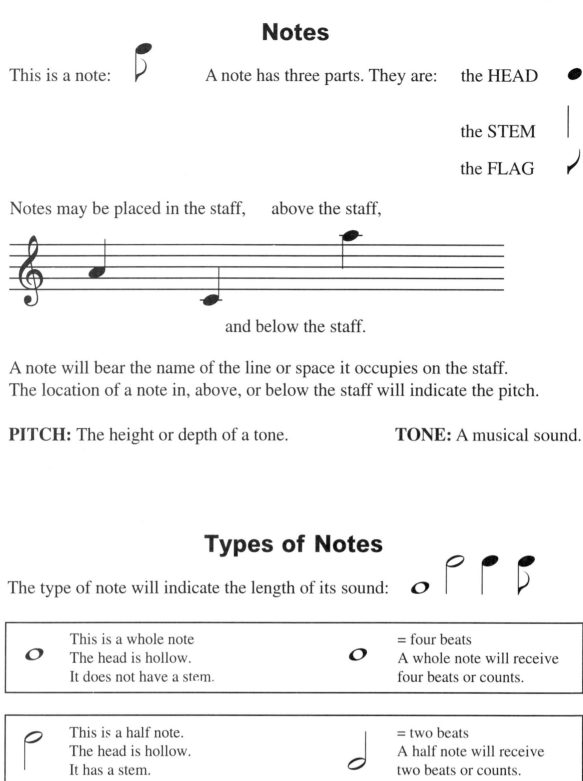

and below the staff.

A note will bear the name of the line or space it occupies on the staff.
The location of a note in, above, or below the staff will indicate the pitch.

PITCH: The height or depth of a tone.   **TONE:** A musical sound.

Types of Notes

The type of note will indicate the length of its sound: 𝅝 ♩ ♩ ♪

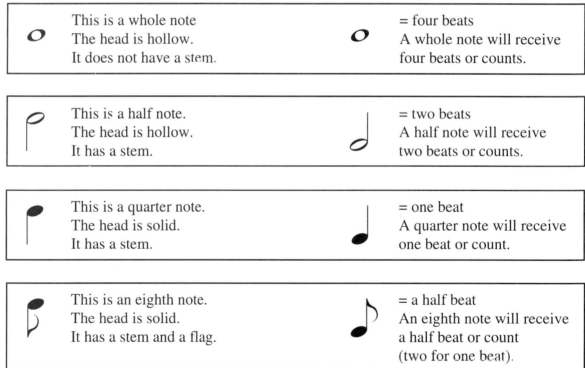

𝅝	This is a whole note. The head is hollow. It does not have a stem.	𝅝 = four beats. A whole note will receive four beats or counts.
𝅗𝅥	This is a half note. The head is hollow. It has a stem.	𝅗𝅥 = two beats. A half note will receive two beats or counts.
♩	This is a quarter note. The head is solid. It has a stem.	♩ = one beat. A quarter note will receive one beat or count.
♪	This is an eighth note. The head is solid. It has a stem and a flag.	♪ = a half beat. An eighth note will receive a half beat or count (two for one beat).

Rests

A REST is a sign used to designate a period of silence. This period of silence will be of the same duration of time as the note to which it corresponds.

𝄾   This is an eighth rest.   𝄽   This is a quarter rest.

▬   This is a half rest. Notice that it lies on the line.

▬   This is a whole rest. Notice that it hangs down from the line. In 3/4 time it also serves as a whole-measure rest.

NOTES

WHOLE 4 COUNTS	HALF 2 COUNTS	QUARTER 1 COUNT	EIGHTH 2 FOR 1 COUNT
▬	▬	𝄽	𝄾

RESTS

48-Bass Accordion

7

The Time Signature

The above examples are the common types of time signatures to be used in this book.

$\frac{4}{4}$ The top number indicates the number of beats per measure.

$\frac{4}{4}$ The bottom number indicates the type of note receiving one beat per measure.

$\frac{4}{4}$ beats per measure.

$\frac{4}{4}$ A quarter note receives one beat.

$\frac{6}{8}$ beats per measure.

$\frac{6}{8}$ Each eighth note receives one full beat.

 Signifies so-called "common time" and is simply another way of designating 4/4 time.

THE LEFT HAND

The left side of the accordion (the side with all the buttons) consists of two types of buttons that produce two types of sounds:

1. BASS BUTTONS that sound only single bass tones which provide standard bass parts, short bass runs, and even bass solos.

2. CHORD BUTTONS that sound several tones at the same time and provide the accompaniment harmony.

On the 120 bass accordion, which is considered the standard accordion, there are 20 diagonal rows. Each of these rows contains 6 buttons. LEARN THESE BUTTONS WELL, as every one of the 20 rows has the same layout, and only the musical pitches change from row to row.

Shown below is the "C" row, generally considered as home-base from which you learn to feel your way to the other rows. The regular "C" bass button will either have a dip or jewel so that you can find it by feel.

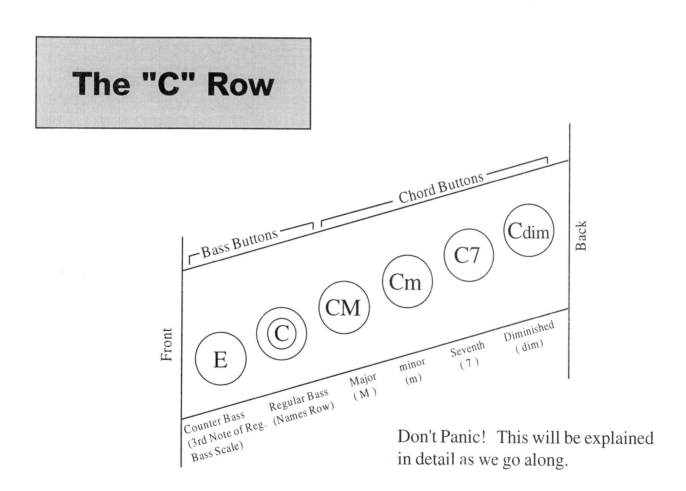

Don't Panic! This will be explained in detail as we go along.

Left-Hand Buttons

𝄢 Bass Clef

In the illustration of the left hand buttons the shaded buttons are the Root Bass Notes that name each diagonal row of 6 buttons.

Remember: The "C" Bass Note is just below the middle of the accordion and is found by feeling for the dip or Jewel.

In each of these 3 rows all buttons are named. All the others are in the same order: M, m, 7, dim, etc.

Some students find it helpful to sit in front of a mirror at first.

Counter Bass Notes Root Bass Notes Major Chords Minor Chords Seventh Chords Diminished Chords

Front

Back

Bottom

10

Right Hand Finger Numbers

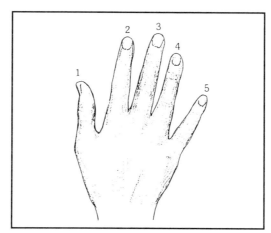

Treble Clef Notes
Right Hand

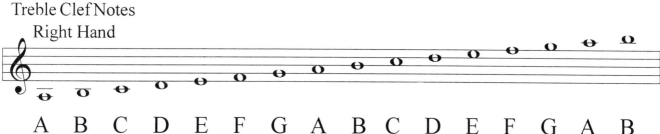

A B C D E F G A B C D E F G A B

Left Hand Finger Numbers

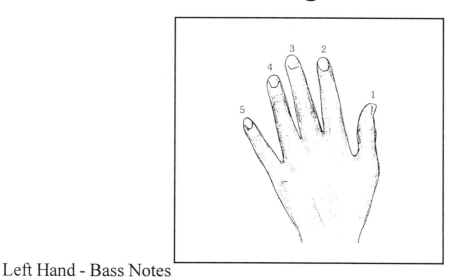

All chords are considered Major (M) unless notated otherwise.
* Example:

C   = C Major
Cm   = C minor
C7   = C seventh
Cdim = C diminished
Note: some books use a "d" to indicate a diminished chord.
Cd = C diminished

Left Hand - Bass Notes

Left Hand - Chords

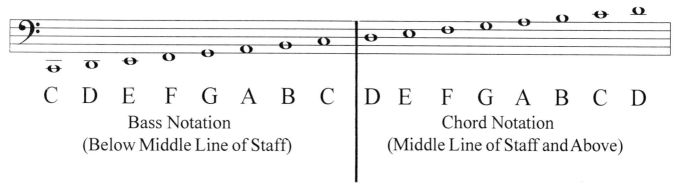

C D E F G A B C │ D E F G A B C D

Bass Notation
(Below Middle Line of Staff)

Chord Notation
(Middle Line of Staff and Above)

Treble Clef

Position of the Notes

The musical alphabet has only seven notes - A, B, C, D, E, F, G - and then it starts over again

A - is to the left of the <u>3rd</u> black key

B - is to the right of the <u>3</u> black keys

C - is to the left of the <u>2</u> black keys

D - is between the <u>2</u> black keys

E - is to the right of the <u>2</u> black keys

F - is to the left of the <u>3</u> black keys

G - is to the right of the first of the <u>3</u> black keys

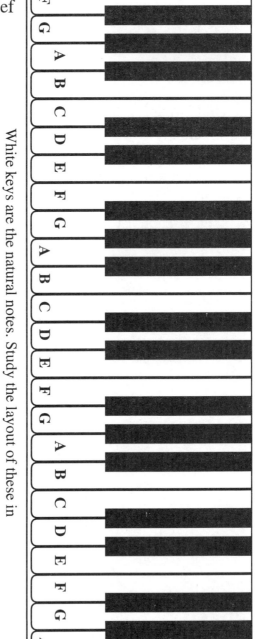

Keyboard of 120 Bass Accordion

Lowest-Sounding Notes
Are at the Top of Accordion

White keys are the natural notes. Study the layout of these in respect to the sets of two black keys and three black keys.

Black keys are the sharps (♯) and flats (♭). This will be explained in detail as needed.

Highest-Sounding Notes
Are at the Bottom of Accordion

FINGERING AND NOTATION GUIDE FOR BOTH HANDS

Learning the "C's"

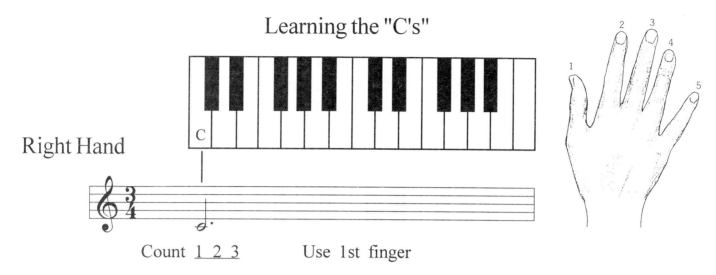

Right Hand

Count 1 2 3   Use 1st finger

"C" is to the left of the two black keys. The note shown above is a dotted quarter note (𝅘𝅥.) which is held for 3 counts. Hold it down and count out loud.

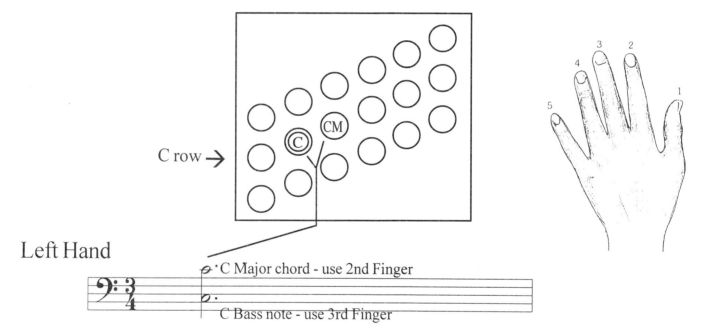

C row →

Left Hand

C Major chord - use 2nd Finger

C Bass note - use 3rd Finger

"C" Bass Note and "C" Major chord. Hold both buttons down (as shown above) and count out loud.

Note:
Fingers should be curved as if holding a ball. Use the tips of the fingers to press the keys.

Putting all the "C's" Together

Remember: ($\boldsymbol{\text{d.}}$) dotted half note = 3 counts ($\boldsymbol{\text{d}}$) half note = 2 counts

($\boldsymbol{\text{d}}$) quarter note = 1 count   (-) whole measure rest

= 3 counts

out = open bellows slowly & steadily
in = close bellows slowly & steadily
* see pages 16 & 26 for more about the bellows

Adding the "G's"

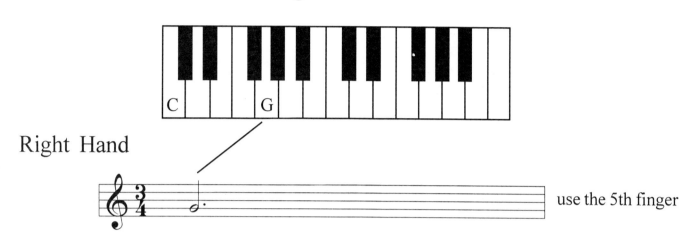

Right Hand

use the 5th finger

"G" is to the right of the 1st of the 3 black keys. Again, hold it down and count.

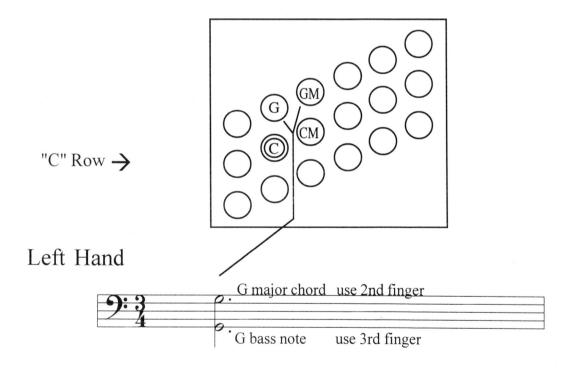

"C" Row →

Left Hand

G major chord   use 2nd finger

G bass note   use 3rd finger

The "G Row" is the next row Above the "C Row". As before, press the G Bass note and G Major chord buttons together, and count.

Proper Use of the Bellows

Open and close the bellows evenly to provide the air to play thje notes – open from the top (like a fan) going in and out about the same distance. Never force the bellows closed – use the air release button which is near the top next to the bass hand strap. Pull a little harder than pushing so that you will not run out of air too soon as you close the bellows.

Mixing the C's and the G's

Bass and Chord Rhythm Drill

Shown below are examples of the most used left hand patterns. Count out loud and practice these exercises regularly until they are even and smooth. Other patterns will be shown as needed.

Three Counts per Measure

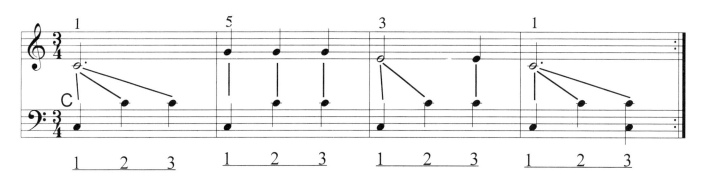

Four Counts per Measure

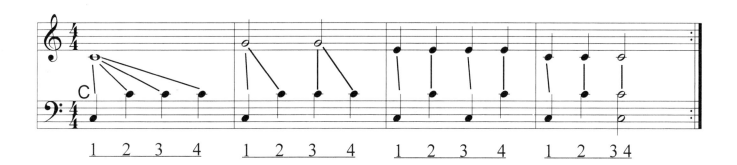

Two Counts per Measure

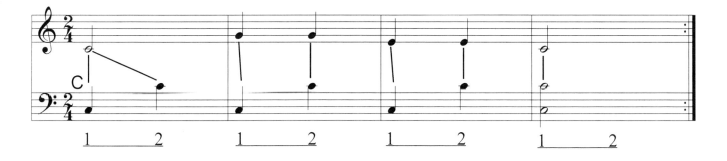

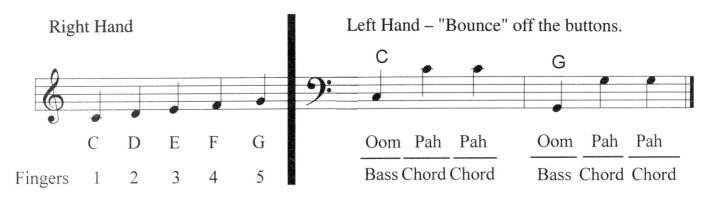

Right Hand

Left Hand – "Bounce" off the buttons.

C   D   E   F   G

Fingers   1   2   3   4   5

Oom	Pah	Pah		Oom	Pah	Pah
Bass	Chord	Chord		Bass	Chord	Chord

Oom-Pah-Pah Waltz

Do not hold bass and chord buttons. Play them short.

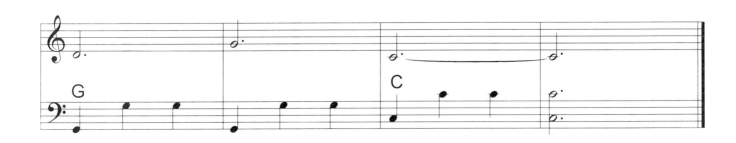

Everybody Has Their Ups and Downs

Practice and count evenly   1 - 2 - 3

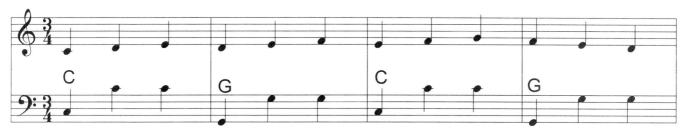

Bass Chord Chord – Remember to play short.

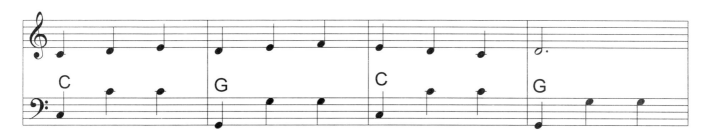

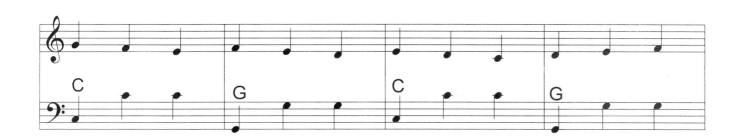

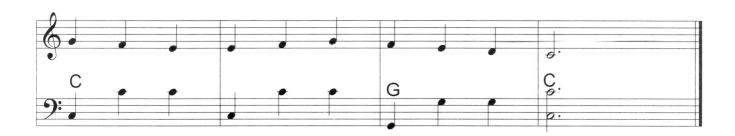

21

The first 5 note pattern you learned $\underline{\text{C D E F G}}$ is called the "C" hand position.

1 2 3 4 5

Shown below is the New "G" hand position. It adds 4 new notes.

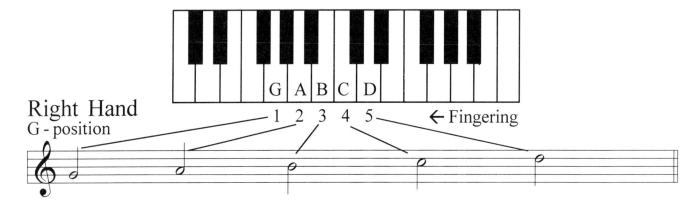

Right Hand
G - position

When playing in different keys the left hand starting position will change. In the example below the left hand will consider the "G" row as the <u>Home Row</u> with the "C" row <u>Below</u> and the new "D" row <u>Above</u>.

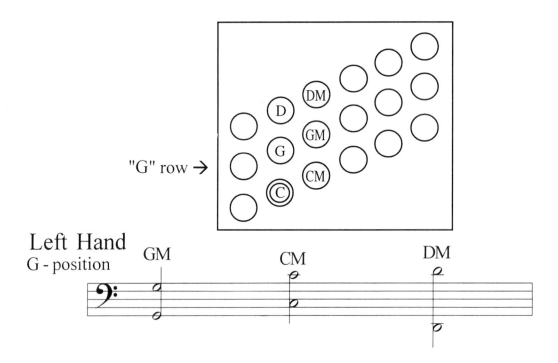

"G" row →

Left Hand
G - position

Déja Vu in G

This song is the same tune as you played before in the "C" position. This time it is played in the "G" position and utilizes the new right hand notes as well as the new left hand "D" bass and chord. Use the fingering shown above the notes.

Children's Song

This song uses 6 notes. The fingering shown will give you some idea of "Common Sense" fingering. *D.C. al Fine*

24

In the example below the eighth notes receive 1/2 count each. (2 played in one count) Count out loud. As shown, the numbers will be the same for the 1st half of every count and "&" will be used for the 2nd half.

NEW BELLOWS HINT - Never change the direction of the bellows in the middle of a note as this will break the sound. There are two reeds for each note - one sounds when opening and another when closing the bellows.

Minuet

Handel

Dotted Quarter Note

A dotted quarter note receives one and a half counts.

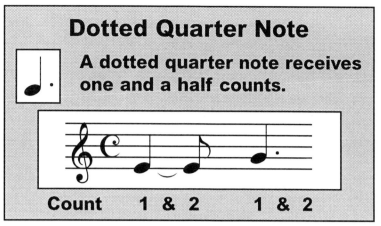

Count   1 & 2   1 & 2

Ode to Joy

Beethoven

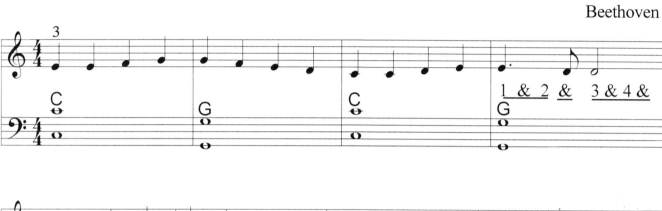

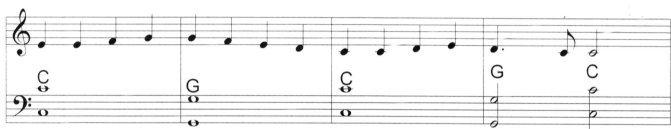

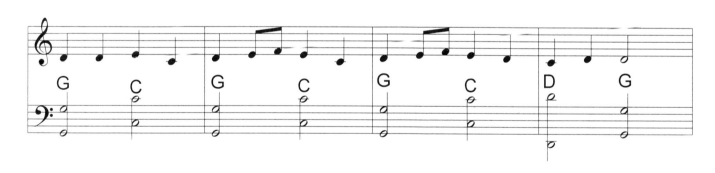

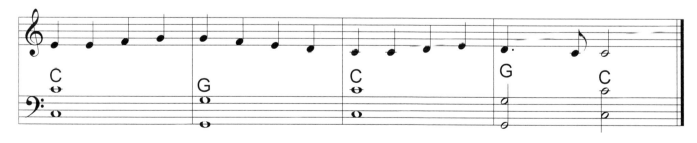

The Slur

A slur is a curved line connecting one or more notes of a different pitch. When a slur occurs, hold each note until the next note is played. Do not lift off before the next note.

Air

Mozart

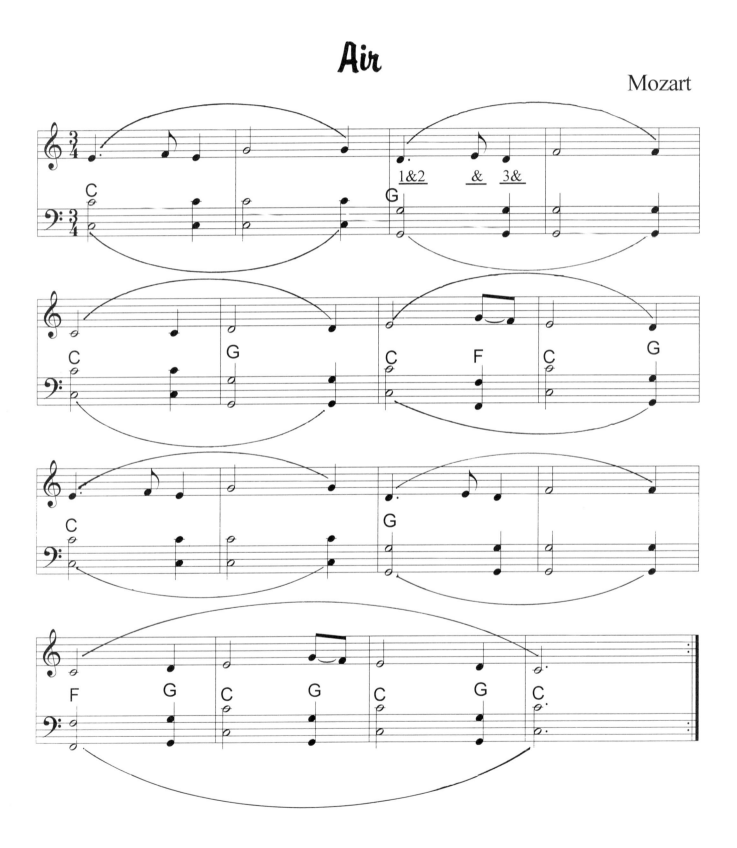

Shown below is a new one-octave (8 notes) higher "C" hand position. This position adds 3 new notes — E, F, G. Compare the sound of these two positions.

Three New Right Hand Notes

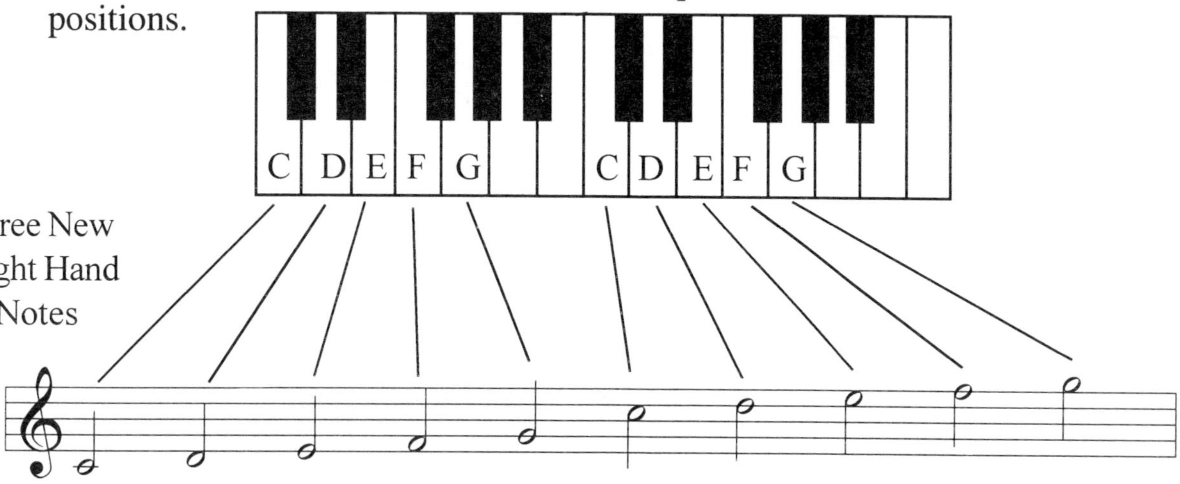

Gavotte

Praetorius

* – Cross 2nd finger over

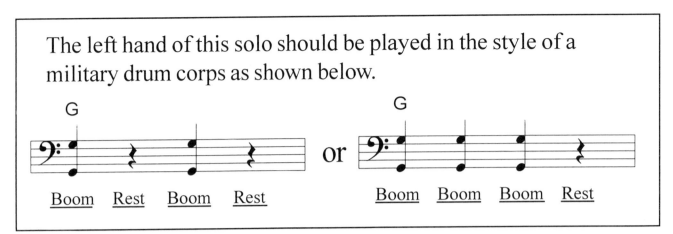

The left hand of this solo should be played in the style of a
military drum corps as shown below.

The British Grenadiers

* Cross over
Note: When two fingerings are shown over the same note (1-2) shift fingers while holding the note down.

Alternating the Bass Notes

Alternating between the bass note that names the chord and the bass note from the next row above helps to make the accompaniment part sound much better. Either the regular or the alternate bass note may be played first. Ex: C bass (c-row), C chord, G bass, (from row above C), the C chord again. The movements are the same no matter which row you are on. These will be referred to as "Bass", "Chord", and "Alternate"

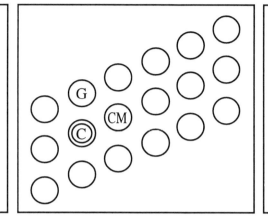

IN 4/4 TIME, PLAY

Bass - Chord
Alternate - Chord

or

Alternate - Chord
Bass - Chord

IN 3/4 TIME, PLAY

Bass - Chord - Chord
Alternate - Chord - Chord

or

Alternate - Chord - Chord
Bass - Chord - Chord

Don't Forget: For single <u>bass</u> buttons and <u>alternate</u> buttons use the 3rd finger — for chord buttons use the 2nd finger.

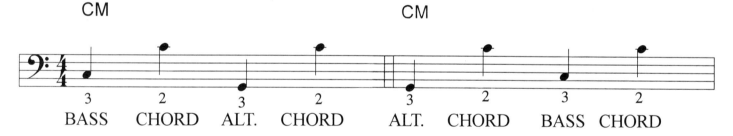

The Triplet

A triplet is a group of three notes played in the time of two notes of the same kind.

is equal to   or   in time value

This famous hymn demonstrates the use of Alternating Bass and the Triplet.

Amazing Grace

Slurs (sometimes called phrases) are like singing. A vocalist will take a breath between phrases. The accordionist will change bellow direction upon starting a phrase.

CHROMATICS

♯ - SHARPS,   ♭ - FLATS, and   ♮ - NATURALS

So far you have used only "Natural" Notes (all white keys), but what about the black ones? They provide tones that are half-steps above and below the white keys that they are adjacent to. There is a whole-step between white keys with two exceptions. It is only a half-step from B to C and E to F, these are the places on the keyboard where there are no black keys between the white keys. See the illustrations below.

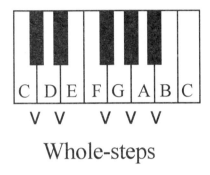

Whole-steps

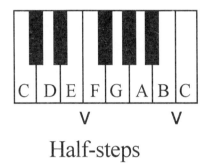

Half-steps

SHARPS

A sharp (♯) placed before a note *raises* its pitch by a half step. A black key has two names possible. Below the notes are named as sharps.

33

A flat (♭) placed before a note *lowers* its pitch by a half step. Below, the same black keys as before are shown and named as flats.

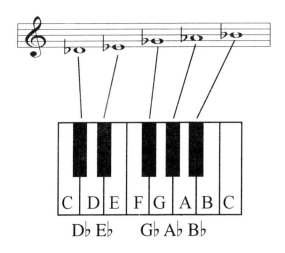

NATURALS

A natural (♮) placed before a note *cancels* a previous sharp or flat. See the explanation below.

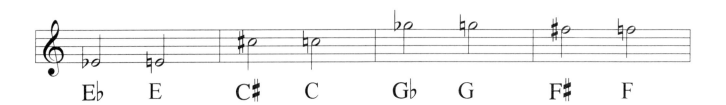

Rule: When a note is changed by an accidental (♯, ♭, or ♮), the accidental remains in effect for *the entire measure* unless it is cancelled by another ♯, ♭, or ♮.

Key Signatures

The key signature will appear at the beginning of a piece. It will show whether there are flats (or sharps) in a song. If a flat appears, all notes of that pitch are flatted unless cancelled by a natural sign (♮).

Shown below are the 1-octave fingerings and the three main chords in each key used in this book.

35

Sustained Bass Notes

In the following solo — hold the bass note for 3 full beats and play the quarter-note chords on beats two and three.

Lullaby

Key of G
F's are sharped

Brahms

This sign is called a fermata. It means to hold the note extra long.

Introducing the Minor Chords

The minor (m) chords are next to the major (M) chords and are played with the same fingering. Remember the single bass notes are played with the 3rd finger and the minor chords will be played with the 2nd finger. The left hand, when using minor chords, works the same in every other respect including alternating the bass notes as shown below.

IN 4/4 TIME, PLAY		**IN 3/4 TIME, PLAY**
Bass - Chord Alternate - Chord or Alternate - Chord Bass - Chord	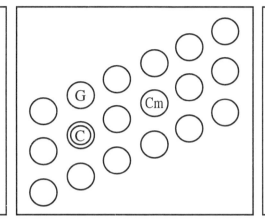	Bass - Chord - Chord Alternate - Chord - Chord or Alternate - Chord - Chord Bass - Chord - Chord

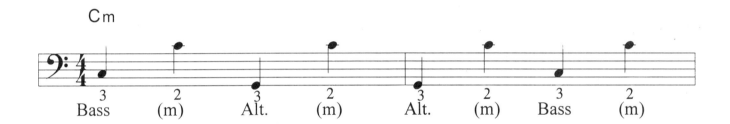

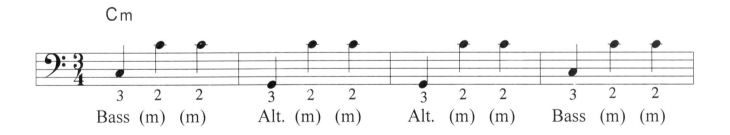

37

Relative Minor Keys

Each major key has a relative minor key that shares the same Key Signature. The minor key starts on the 6th note of the major scale. The major key signatures that are used in this book are shown below with their relative minor keys. If you are not sure about the key you are in you can usually tell by the name of the last melody note or final chord.

No sharps or flats

Key of C Major   OR   Key of A Minor

One sharp (F♯)

Key of G Major   OR   Key of E Minor

Two sharps (F♯ & C♯)

Key of D Major   OR   Key of B Minor

One flat (B♭)

Key of F Major   OR   Key of D Minor

Two flats (B♭ & E♭)

Key of B♭ Major   OR   Key of G Minor

Hungarian Dance #4

Key of A Minor

Brahms

Introducing the 7th Chords

The 7th chords (7) are next to the minor (m) chords and are played with the same fingering. The alternating bass notes work the same with the Major (M), minor (m), and the 7th (7) chords. Single bass notes are played with the 3rd finger and the chords are played with the 2nd finger.

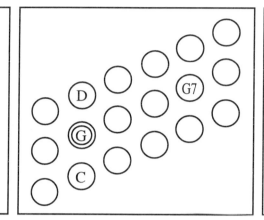

IN 4/4 TIME, PLAY

Bass - Chord
Alternate - Chord

or

Alternate - Chord
Bass - Chord

IN 3/4 TIME, PLAY

Bass - Chord - Chord
Alternate - Chord - Chord

or

Alternate - Chord - Chord
Bass - Chord - Chord

G7

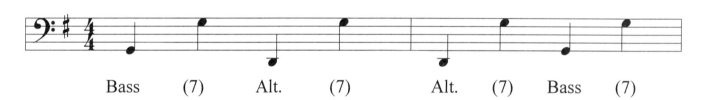

Bass   (7)   Alt.   (7)   Alt.   (7)   Bass   (7)

G7

Bass   (7) (7)   Alt. (7) (7)   Alt. (7) (7)   Bass (7) (7)

The God of Abraham Praise

Key of G Minor (B♭ & E♭)

Hebrew

* Thumb (1) under.

Skaters Waltz

Key of C
This tune demonstrates
the use of the minor (m) chord

French Song

Key of G Minor (B♭ & E♭)

Tschaikovsky

Sur le Pont d'Avignon

This tune demonstrates the
use of the 7th chord
Key of G

French

Wandering

Key of G Minor (B♭ & E♭)

Neil Griffin

The Bells of St. Marys

Sixteenth Notes

A sixteenth note looks like this

Several sixteenth notes together look like this

A sixteenth rest looks like this: It takes 2 sixteenth notes to equal 1 eighth note, or 4 sixteenth notes to equal 1 quarter note.

Eighth Rest

An eighth rest receives the same time value as an eighth note.

Polka, Polka

Key of C

Neil Griffin

Are You From Dixie

Key of C

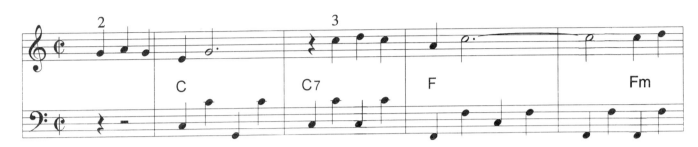

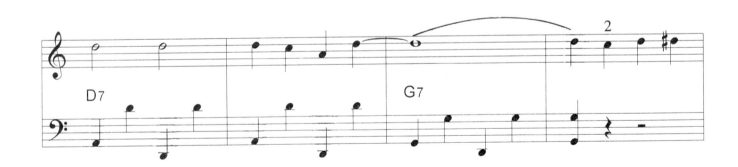

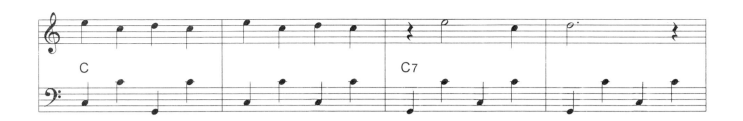

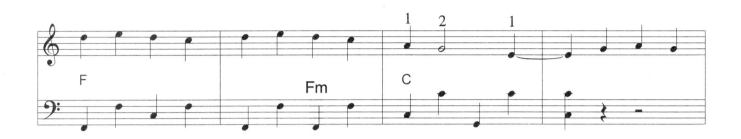

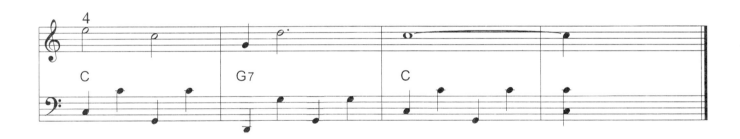

Grace Notes

Grace notes are used in Cajun tunes quite a bit. The time is very short and is actually "robbed" from the note it is attached to. The use of grace notes gives the impression that you are "sliding" into the note....

Lake Charles Waltz

Cajun

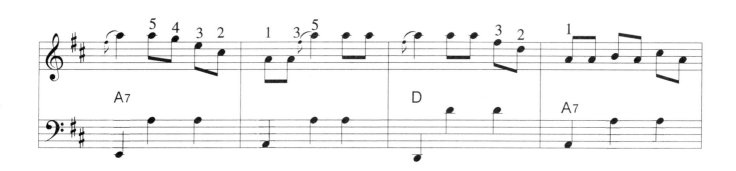

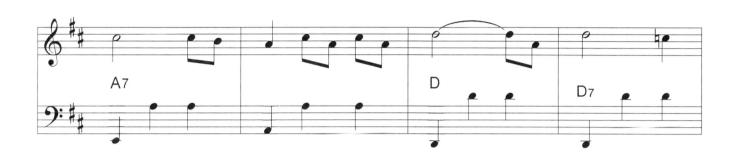

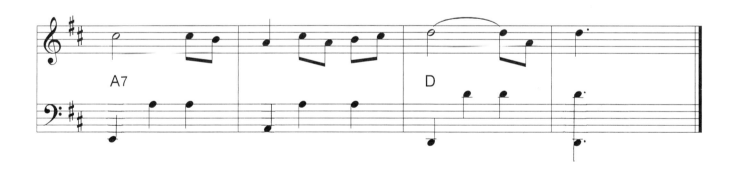

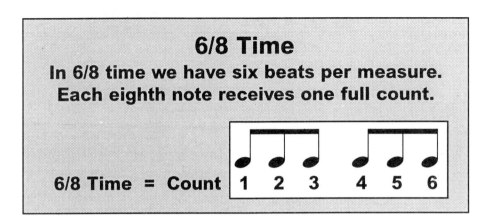

6/8 Time
In 6/8 time we have six beats per measure.
Each eighth note receives one full count.

6/8 Time = Count | 1 2 3   4 5 6

Key of G

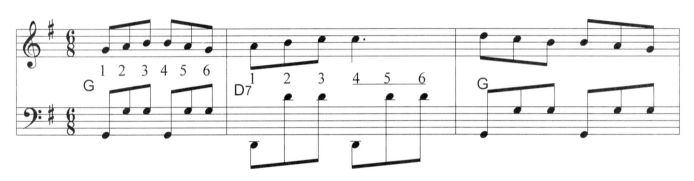

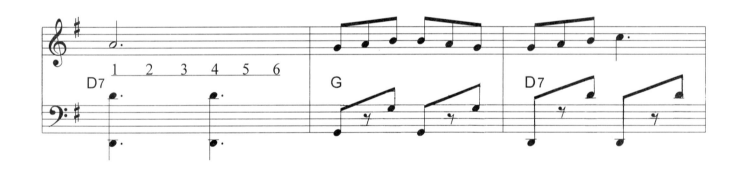

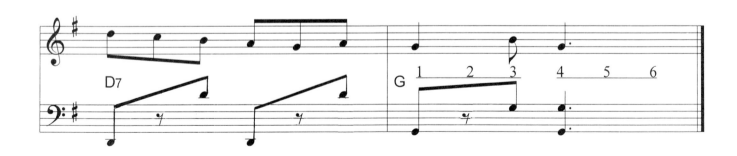

When Johnny Comes Marching Home

Key of A minor

Come Back to Sorrento

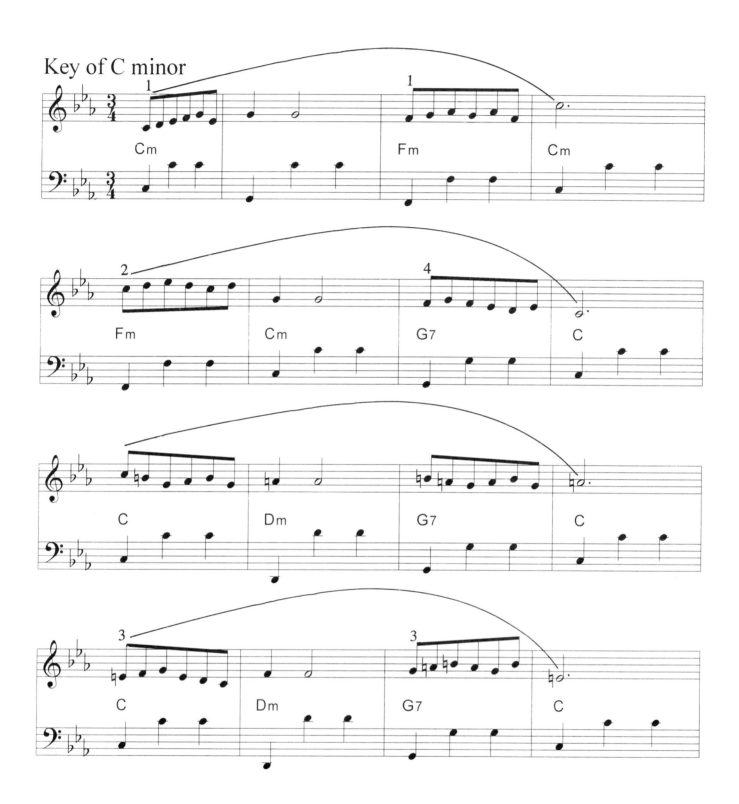

* Ritard = slow down gradually

Dotted Eighths and Sixteenths

A dotted eighth note followed by a sixteenth note is a common figure in music. Practice the following study until it is felt and understood.

Two Steppin' 'Cross Texas

Key of G

Neil Griffin

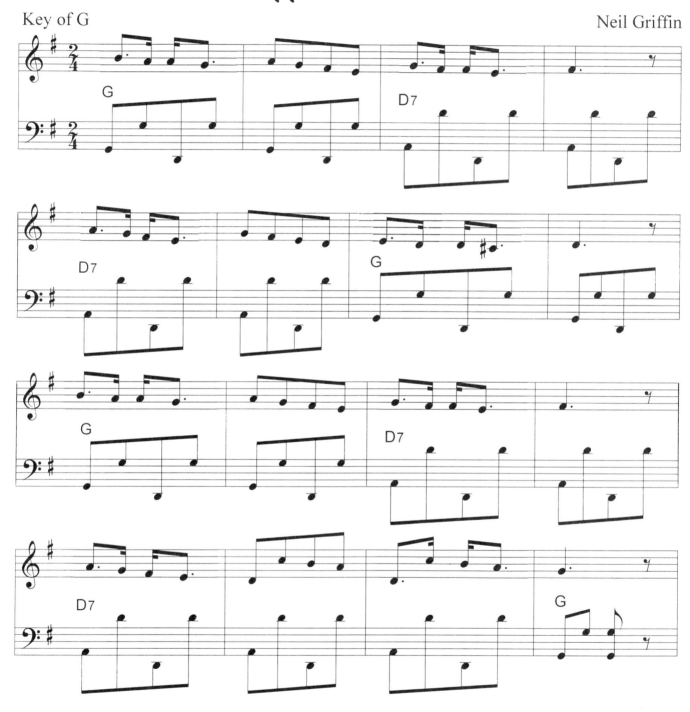

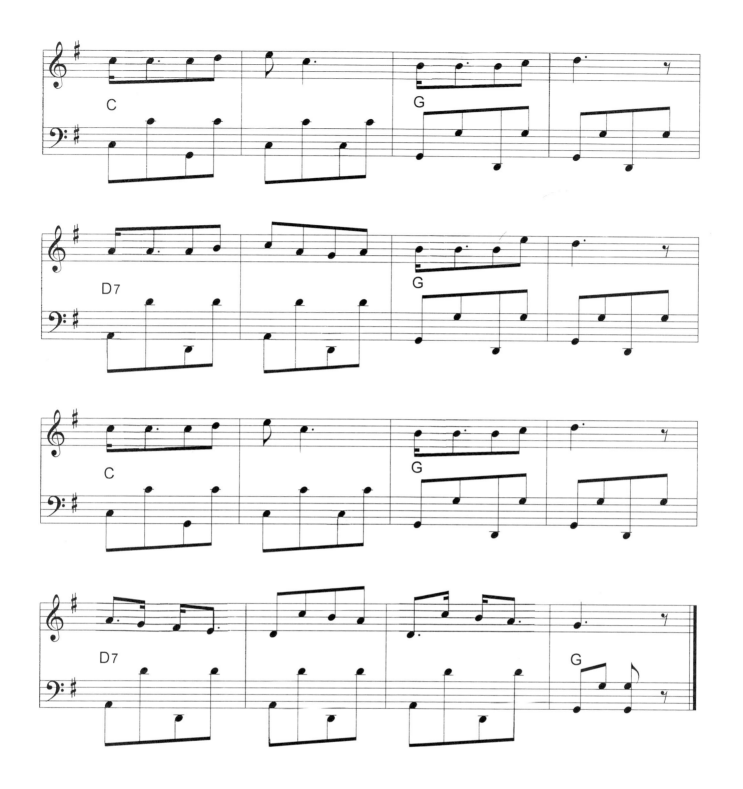

Julida Polka

Intro

Staccato

When a dot is placed under or over a note (♩) this means to play the note as if it were only half its value followed by a rest equal to half of its value.

Legato

When a dash is placed under or over a note (♩) in the right hand it means to give the note its full value and to connect to the next note with no space in between.

Andante

Key of F

Haydn

59

Jambalaya

Cajun

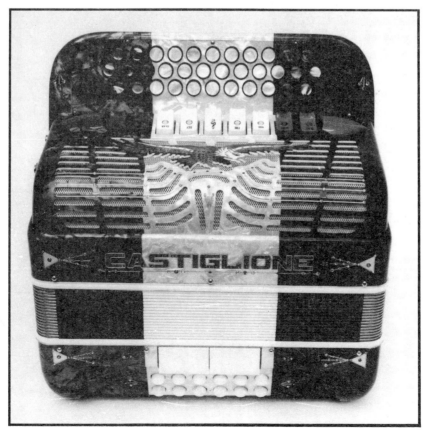

Vienna-Style Accordion

Pretty Fair Maid Jig

Peg O' My Heart

Rattle the Bottles Reel

Rick's Reel

Introducing the Counter-Bass Notes

The single tone, "Counter-Bass" Buttons add the ability to play scales, runs, and solos in the left hand bass parts.

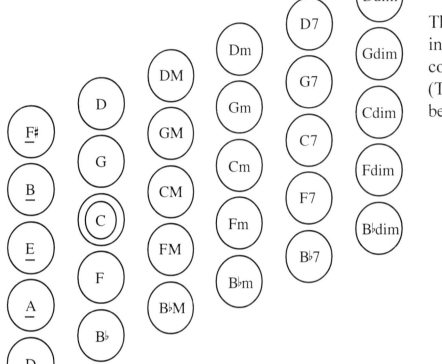

The underlined buttons in this diagram are the counter-bass notes. (The row closest to the bellows)

Shown below is the musical notation for basses and counter-basses from the above diagram. You already know the regular basses - notice that a counter bass is always <u>underlined</u>

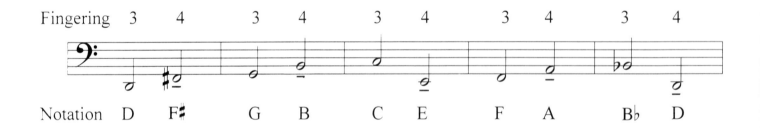

In the next several pages we will combine the regular- bass buttons with the counter-bass buttons and chords to produce a better sounding and more interesting left hand part.

Shown below are a few examples of location and notation of counter-basses.

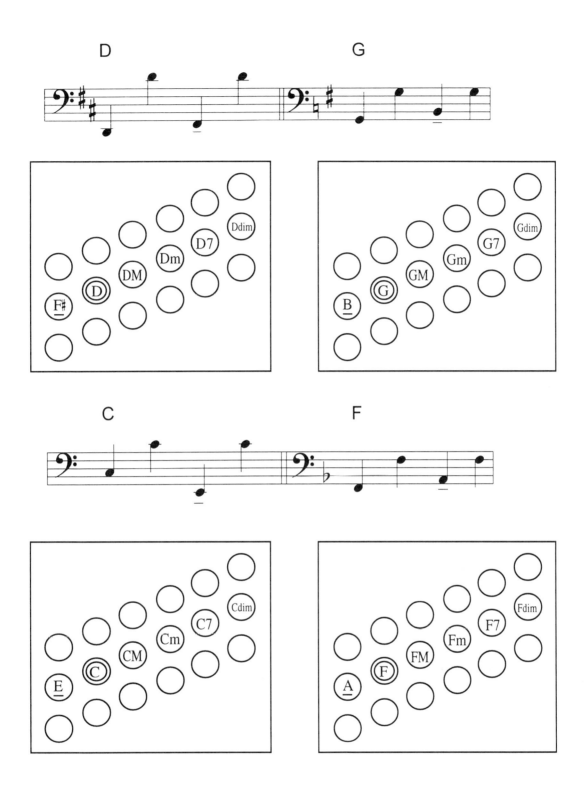

THE LEFT HAND EXERCISES BELOW WILL HELP YOU BEGIN TO SEE SOME OF THE WAYS THAT THE COUNTER-BASS NOTES ARE USED.........

March

Key of C

Handel

Introducing the Diminished Chords

The last row of chord buttons contains the diminished (dim) chords and is found next to the seventh (7) chord row. The diminished chord is a passing or connecting type chord and the alternate bass patterns are not used as with the **M**, **m**, & **7** chords. The bass note is usually the same name and is on the same row as the diminished chord or is the counter-bass from 3 rows above as shown in the examples below.

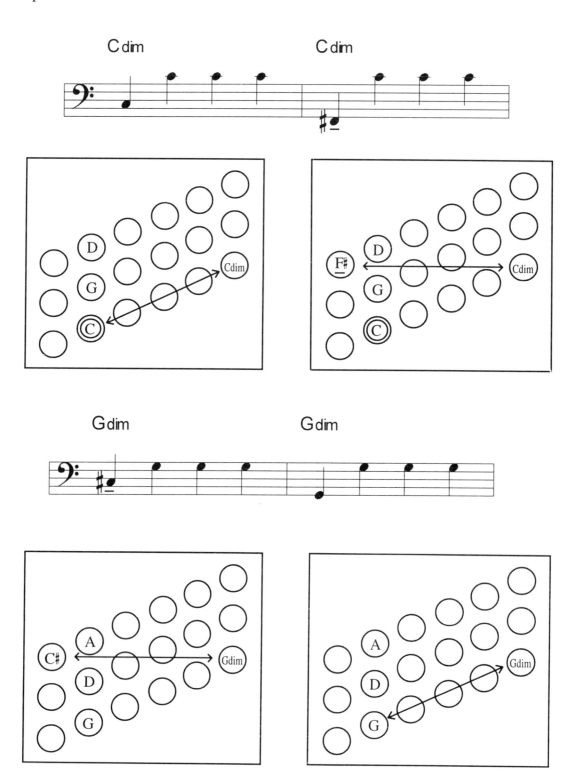

Ja-da

Chinatown

Key of C

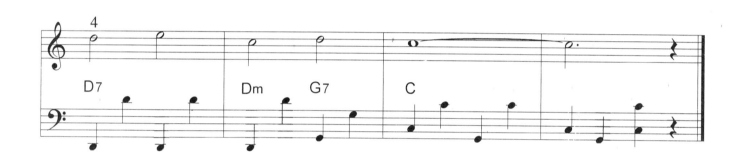

Cajun Accordion

I Want a Girl, Just Like the Girl
(That Married Dear Old Dad)

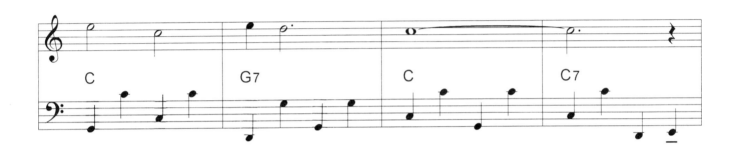

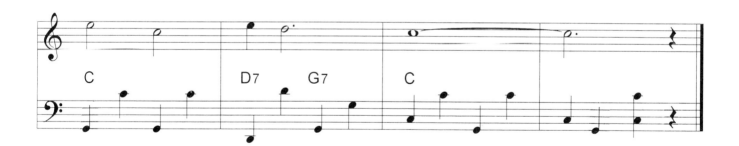

I Love You Truly

Key of C

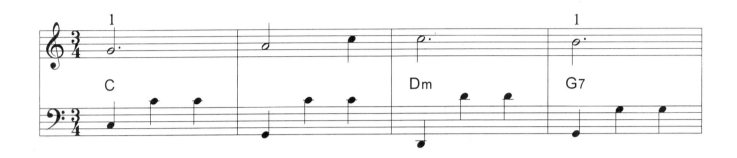

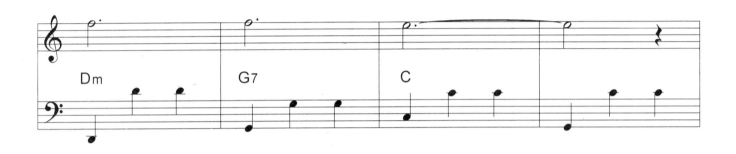

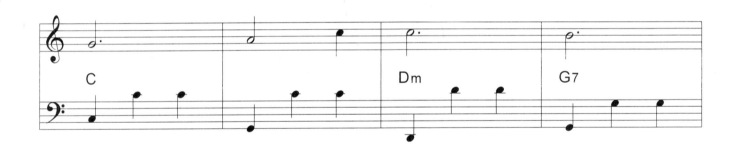

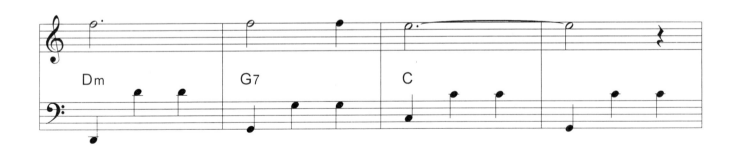

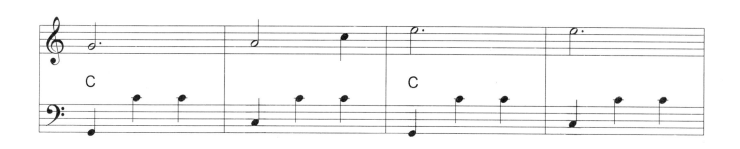

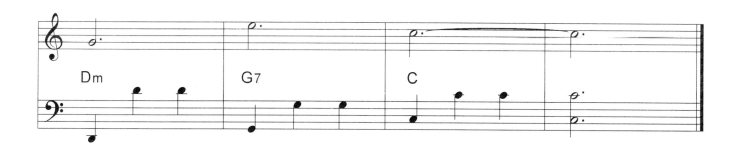

Smiles

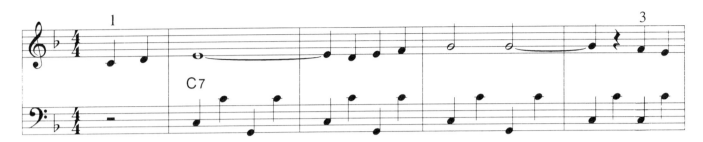

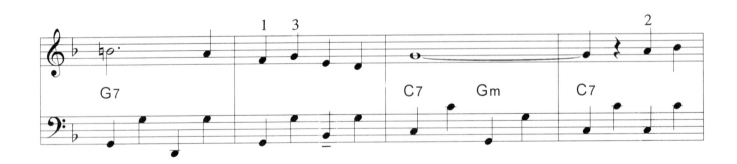

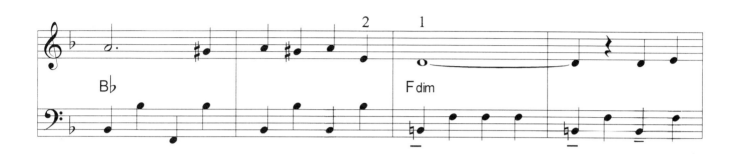

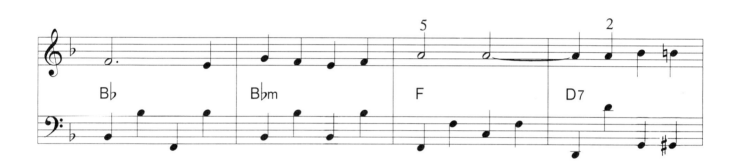

For Me and My Gal

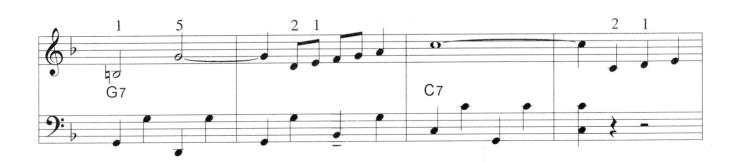

Washington and Lee Swing

Key of C

Fascination

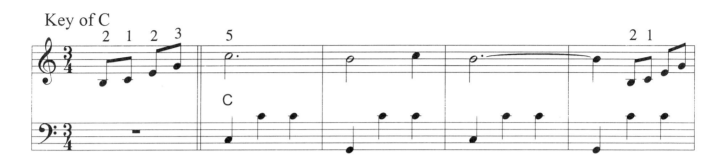

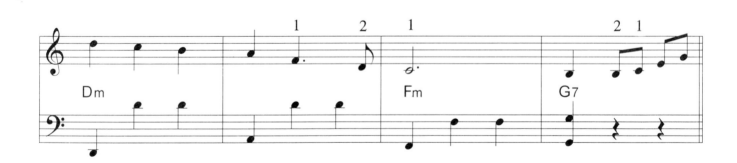

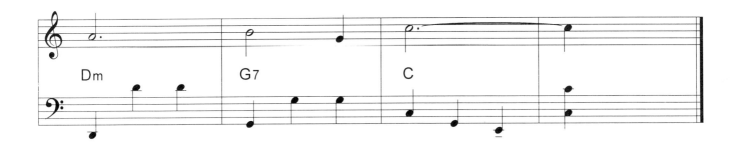

El Capitan March

Key of C

Sousa

Sweetheart of Sigma Chi

Key of C

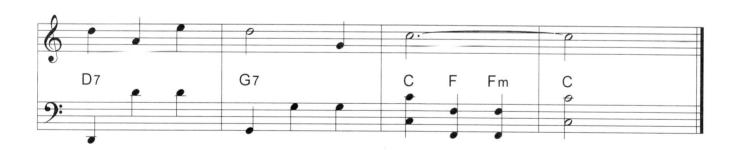

Melancholy Baby

Key of D

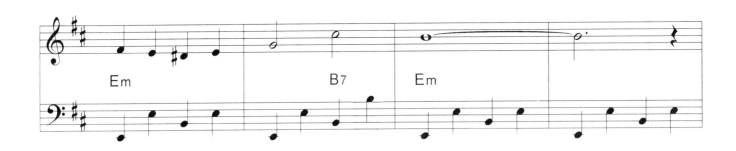

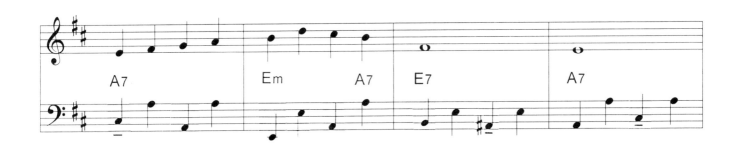

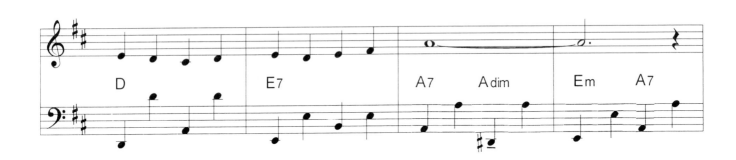

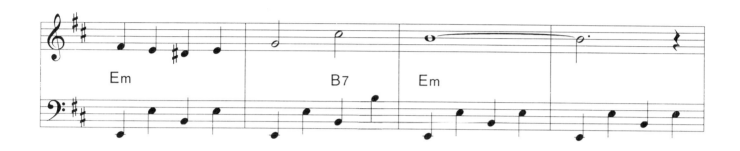

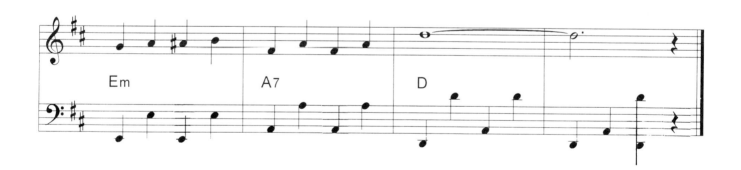

RIGHT-HAND HARMONY

The use of 3rds (3 notes apart) and 6ths (6 notes apart) provides easy and pleasing harmony sounds in right-hand parts. This is included here to demonstrate how 3rds and 6ths are used.

El Caballo Bayo

Mexican

Mexican Siesta

Neil Griffin

Key of C

BASS AND CHORD BUTTON REVIEW

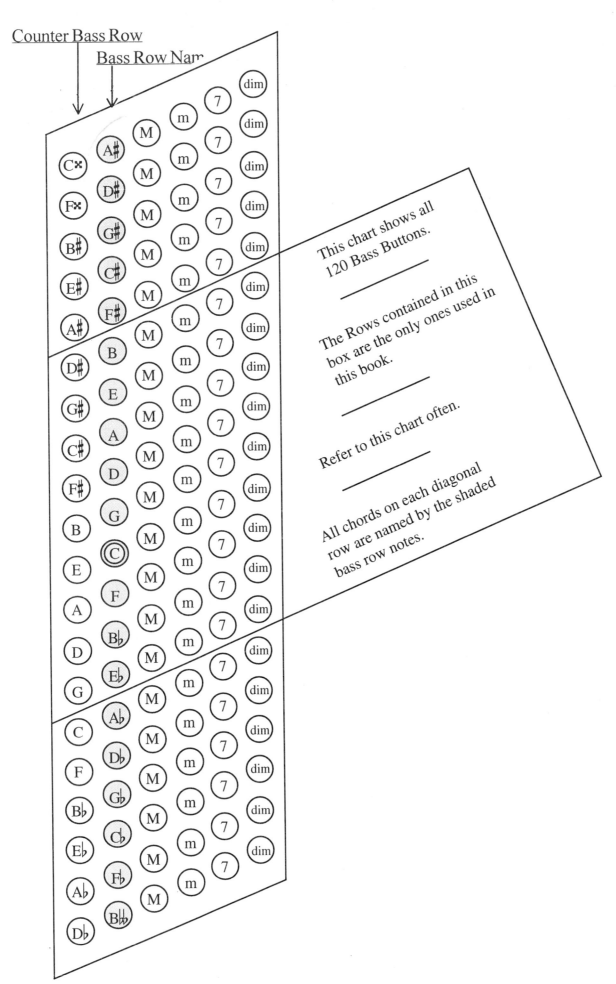

Counter Bass Row

Bass Row Name

This chart shows all 120 Bass Buttons.

The Rows contained in this box are the only ones used in this book.

Refer to this chart often.

All chords on each diagonal row are named by the shaded bass row notes.